The Development of U.S. Industry

by Mary Meinking

MG (4-8)
ATOS 4.8
1.0 pts
Non-Fiction

146879 EN

D1203779

LANGUAGE ARTS EXPLORER

THE DEVELOPMENT OF U.S. INDUSTRY

1870 to 1900

by Mary Meinking

HISTORY DIGS

CHERRY LAKE PUBLISHING • ANN ARBOR, MICHIGAN

Published in the United States of America
by Cherry Lake Publishing
Ann Arbor, Michigan
www.cherrylakepublishing.com

Printed in the United States of America
Corporate Graphics Inc
September 2011
CLFA09

Consultants: Brett Barker, associate professor of history, University of Wisconsin –
Marathon County; Gail Saunders-Smith, associate professor of literacy, Beeghly College of
Education, Youngstown State University

Editorial direction:
Rebecca Rowell

Series design and cover production:
Marie Tupy

Interior production:
Emily Love

Photo credits: Currier & Ives/Library of Congress, cover, 1; iStockphoto, 5, 17; AP Images, 6,
16, 18, 25; Andrew J. Russell/AP Images, 7; North Wind Picture Archives, 9, 21; Anton Foltin/
iStockphoto, 10; A. Loeffler, Tompkinsville, NY/Library of Congress, 12; Augustus Sherman/AP
Images, 13; Alexander Graham Bell/Library of Congress, 23; Shutterstock Images, 27; Stuart
Miles/Shutterstock Images, 30

Library of Congress Cataloging-in-Publication Data
Meinking, Mary, 1958-
 The development of US industry / by Mary Meinking.
    p. cm. – (Language arts explorer–History digs)
 ISBN 978-1-61080-198-0 – ISBN 978-1-61080-286-4 (pbk.)
 1. Industries–United States–History–Juvenile literature. 2. Industries–United States–Juvenile
literature. 3. Industrial revolution–United States–History–Juvenile literature. I. Title. II. Title:
Development of U.S. industry.
 HC105.6.M37 2011
 338.0973–dc22
                                           2011015123

**Cherry Lake Publishing would like to acknowledge the work of The Partnership for 21st
Century Skills. Please visit www.21stCenturySkills.org for more information.**

TABLE OF CONTENTS

You are being given a mission. The facts in What You Know will help you accomplish it. Remember the clues from What You Know while you are reading the story. The clues and the story will help you answer the questions at the end of the book. Have fun on this adventure!

YOUR MISSION

Your mission is to learn to think like a historian. What tools do historians use to research the past? What kinds of questions do they ask, and where do they look for answers? On this assignment, your goal is to investigate how the United States became the industrial leader of the world at the dawn of the twentieth century. Who helped change the country, and in what ways? How did new technology unite the East and West Coasts? How did the lives of American Indians change during this time? Be sure to remember facts from What You Know as you read.

WHAT YOU KNOW

★ The **transcontinental** railroad joined the East and West Coasts.

★ The U.S. government took land long inhabited by American Indians.

★ The United States had an open door policy—almost anyone, from anywhere, could immigrate.

★ The invention of the telephone changed the way people communicated.

Use this book to explore history in ways a historian might. A student researched this period of U.S. history while on a summer road trip. Carry out your mission by reading the student's travel journal.

The Statue of Liberty was a symbol of hope for millions of immigrants who came to the United States during its immigration boom.

We started our summer trip today. We're heading around the country to visit Mom's old college classmates. She's a college history professor and her friends are history buffs too. What a way to spend my summer vacation . . . in a van with my little brother! At least Mom gave me this awesome travel journal to keep track of our trip. I'm excited to learn more about history all around the country.

Promontory Summit

Today, we arrived at the Golden **Spike** National Historic Site in Promontory Summit, Utah. Ben, my brother, is so excited to see the trains. Mom introduced us to Hank Sampson, her friend. He works at the visitor's center and showed us around. We stopped under a big map of the United States. "What do you think this map shows?" he asked us.

"It looks like a giant spider web over there," Ben said, pointing.

"That's not a spider web," I said. "That's all the railroads in the East and only one in the West."

"Right," Hank said. "Before 1869, there was no railroad connecting the coasts. It took up to six months to go from New York to San Francisco by land or water. Citizens wanted a transcontinental railroad. The government approved the building of the transcontinental railroad in 1862."

"That was during the Civil War. Didn't the war get in the way of building the railroad?" I asked.

Photographs are valuable artifacts. This one shows how railroad workers at Promontory Summit, Utah, celebrated completing the first transcontinental railroad line in the United States.

"It did," he said. "But there were lots of soldiers without jobs after the war. They joined the Irish and Chinese immigrants to build the railroad. The Union Pacific Railroad built the track from Omaha, Nebraska, heading west. The Central Pacific Railroad built the track from Sacramento, California, heading east. The companies competed to lay the most track. The government gave the railroads land and money for every mile of track they laid."

"And the two tracks met here?" I asked.

"Yes! And it was something to celebrate. As the last spike was stuck, a telegraph message 'D-O-N-E' was sent from coast to coast. The United States celebrated!"

"So, after the railroad was done, how fast could people go from coast to coast?" I asked.

"It took only seven days," Hank said. "But even more important was how quickly goods could move from place to place. The railroad helped suppliers all over the nation sell their goods nationwide."

"Shall we go watch the trains?" Hank asked.

"That's a great idea," Mom said. "Thanks for the tour, Hank! It was good to see you again." ★

OTHER TRANSCONTINENTAL RAILROADS

The United States later had other transcontinental railroads, including the Great Northern, Northern Pacific, Santa Fe, Southern, and Milwaukee. Other countries have transcontinental railroads as well. With a last spike ceremony in 1885, the Canadian Pacific Railway connected British Columbia to Montreal. Russian soldiers and prisoners completed the Trans-Siberian Railroad in 1916.

After driving for a day, we arrived at the Indian Museum of North America. We're in the Black Hills of South Dakota. Dr. Jane Morning Star, Mom's friend, is the museum curator.

Losing the Buffalo

"Welcome! Let me show you some pieces of American Indian life. You might be interested in this," she said unfolding a furry animal skin. "What do you think this is?"

"A bear skin rug?" Ben asked, petting it.

"No, it's buffalo," she said. "What do you think this has to do with American Indians?"

"Indians ate buffalo," I said.

"Right. They also used the buffalo hides for clothes and shelter," she replied. "Indians only killed as many buffalo as they needed. The Indians followed the buffalo herds across the plains."

"Didn't there used to be millions of buffalo?" I asked.

"Yes, there were an estimated 60 million buffalo in North America when Christopher Columbus landed here in 1492," Jane said. "But white settlers changed that. Trappers and traders killed buffalo to sell their hides and meat. During the winter of 1872-1873, more than 1.5 million hides were shipped east. And when the transcontinental railroad came through the area, buffalo got in the way. On some trains, travelers were allowed to shoot buffalo.

The North American buffalo, or bison, was central to American Indians' way of life until white settlers killed millions of the animals.

The railroad companies also hired hunters to kill them. They also held buffalo killing contests. The scout and showman Buffalo Bill killed thousands of buffalo, shooting more than 4,000 in 18 months. By 1900, there were only about 1,000 buffalo left!"

Losing Their Land

"I feel sorry for the buffalo," I said. "But didn't the American Indians lose more than the buffalo? Didn't they lose land?"

"Yes, they were pushed off their **ancestral** lands and forced westward as more whites arrived," Jane said. "When the transcontinental railroad went through, the U.S. government gave away millions of acres of Indian land."

"I bet they were upset to lose it," I said.

"Yes, they were!" Jane replied. "The tribes fought for their land. Many people—American Indians and whites—were killed. The American Indians were outnumbered, and the whites had more gun power. The government signed treaties with the American Indians and let them keep some land. However, if it turned out to be good farmland or gold or oil were discovered on the land, tribes would get moved again."

"That doesn't seem fair," I said.

"Sadly, that's what happened," she said. "In 1887, the government passed the Dawes Act. That split up the Indian **reservations** into smaller individual plots of land. The government wanted the Indians to become farmers."

"Did they grow their own food?" I asked.

"No, the land wasn't good for farming. No crops grew," Jane said. "Plus, many American Indians were hunters, not farmers. They went hungry. The government gave them food in exchange for more of their land. Tribes were pushed onto smaller and smaller reservations."

"I want to see the arrowhead collection," Ben begged.

"Okay, I'll let you guys wander around. I've got to get back to work," Jane said. "Thanks for coming to visit, Elisabeth. Nice to meet you guys!"

We waved good-bye and finished looking at the museum. ★

THE NAVAJO NATION

The largest reservation in the United States is the Navajo Nation. Its 17 million acres cover parts of Utah, Arizona, and New Mexico. On the reservation, many women weave rugs and many men make jewelry to sell. The Navajo have found natural gas, oil, coal, and uranium on the reservation, which bring in millions of dollars each year.

After three days on the road, we arrived in New York City to see another of Mom's friends. We rode the ferry to Ellis Island in New York Harbor. Jimmy Grant, a historian there, met us at the dock and showed us around.

Looking for a Better Life

"Immigration to the United States boomed after 1880," Jimmy said. "Most Europeans came to the United States to escape starvation and oppressive rulers. Others came to seek religious freedom, to find good jobs, or to make money. European farmers came when the transcontinental railroad advertised cheap land in the West. The Castle Garden Immigration Station in New York,

Ellis Island was a welcomed sight for the thousands of immigrants who traveled a long way to the United States from their homelands.

across the harbor, was the first official center for immigration," Jimmy said, pointing, "but it wasn't able to handle the 8 million people who poured into the United States."

"Was that when they started entering the country through Ellis Island?" I asked.

"Yes, more than 12 million immigrants entered the country through Ellis Island between 1892 and 1954," Jimmy told us. "On average, 5,000 people came through here every day. Their names were recorded. The immigrants were asked their age, where they were going, and what their **calling**, or job, was. Next, they had to be checked by doctors to verify they were physically and mentally well."

"Was it possible to be turned away?" I asked.

"Yes, but only 2 percent of people were sent back home," he said.

We walked around and saw rooms filled with old suitcases, shoes, and clothes.

"Why are all these things here?" I asked.

"The immigrants carried their belongings with them on the ships. I think these things simply got too heavy to carry or were forgotten here," Jimmy said.

A Challenging Life

"Where did they go after they left Ellis Island?" I asked.

"They spread out all over the country," he said. "Many went to live and work with family or friends in cramped big city **tenements**. Others found jobs in mills, factories, or mines, or worked for the

BECOMING A U.S. CITIZEN

It's much harder to immigrate to the United States today than it was years ago. Foreigners have several ways they can become citizens. The quickest way is to marry an American or have an American parent or child. Another way is to get a good job in the United States. Scientists with special skills and people who invest a great deal of money in the United States also can become citizens. Becoming a citizen can take only a few months to many years.

railroad. Some immigrants headed west to farm. Here's a photo of some immigrants working," he said, handing me a photograph.

"What are those kids doing?" I asked.

"They are doing piece work, making paper flowers to sell. Most fathers' jobs paid very little. Mothers of young children worked at home to make extra money. Their children helped them do the work. Some made flowers, clothes, or cigars. Others cracked nuts and pulled out the meats. Children as young as two helped," Jimmy said. "Families made only pennies for every 144 flowers they made. Pay ranged from 3.5 cents to 25 cents, depending on the type of flower."

"So, immigrants came to the United States because life was bad in their home countries," I said. "But it sounds like they had to struggle to survive here."

"Yes, they did," Jimmy said. After visiting a while longer, Jimmy walked us back to the ferry dock. "Good to see you, Elisabeth," he said. "Come back to visit us again, kids!" ★

Today, we visited another part of New York City. We met Scott Stanley at the Brooklyn Bridge. He's a metals historian.

"Hi, Elisabeth!" he said, hugging Mom. "Good to see you. I hear you guys wanted to find out more about the steel industry. I've got just the thing to show you," he said, sitting on the bench and patting it for us to join him. "Kids, do you know what this is?" he asked, showing us a photograph.

The Appeal of Steel

"Is that a giant Easter egg?" Ben asked.

"No, this was the way they used to make steel," he said. "Inside that giant container, air blew through melted iron to remove **impurities** such as carbon, silicon, and manganese. The impurities escaped into the air or formed slag, a solid waste that was easy to separate from the liquid steel. This process is named after Sir Henry

RECYCLED STEEL

In North America today, almost 69 percent of all steel is recycled. That's more than 80 million tons of steel every year. That steel comes from food cans, old buildings, and cars. The average American uses 142 steel cans, such as soup or pasta cans, every year. Steel cans are the most recycled food containers—600 every second! Recycling steel saves enough energy to power 18 million homes for an entire year.

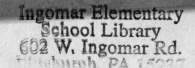

Bessemer of England, who developed and patented it there. The process was a quick and cheap way to turn iron into steel. Steel was flexible yet strong enough to be used for railroad ties, bridges, and steel building frames."

"So, were the railroad ties and rails used on the transcontinental railroad made of steel?" I asked.

"No, most of the metal used in the transcontinental railroad was iron. The railroad was built before the Bessemer process was used in the United States. In 1860, the country lagged behind Great Britain, France, and Germany in making steel. But an immigrant named Andrew Carnegie saw steel made near London using the Bessemer

Andrew Carnegie made millions of dollars in the steel industry.

method. He built the first U.S. steel plants to use the process. His company made tons of steel and millions of dollars," Scott said. "By 1900, the United States made more steel than those other countries combined!"

"That must be why so many things were made of steel," I said.

The Brooklyn Bridge

"Yes," he said. "That was the U.S. steel boom. Let's walk across the Brooklyn Bridge and I'll show you some more uses for steel."

"Yippie! Let's go!" Ben said, running ahead of us. We walked to the top of the bridge for a great view of the Empire State Building and Statue of Liberty.

"What do you think those are?" Scott asked, pointing to the cables holding up the bridge.

"Really thick ropes," I answered.

"They're steel wires twisted together," he explained. "The bridge's designer, John Roebling, wove steel wires together to make strong steel cables. The cables allow the bridge to span the river. This was the first **suspension bridge** to use steel cables. It was also the longest suspension bridge in the world when it was completed in 1883. Why do you think this bridge was important to New Yorkers?"

"Because it connected the island of Manhattan to most of New York," I said.

"That's right," Scott said. "Many people worked in Manhattan but lived in Brooklyn. Before the bridge was built, people and goods

Planners and workers met on the Brooklyn Bridge during construction of the historic structure.

traveled back and forth by ferry every day. But the ferries couldn't run during the winter when the East River was frozen. Once the Brooklyn Bridge opened, people poured over the bridge. More than 150,000 people used the bridge on opening day!"

"We'd better catch up with Ben," Mom said. "Thanks for the info, Scott. It was good to see you again!" We jogged to catch up with Ben and finished walking across the bridge. ★

Our next stop was in Pennsylvania. Today, we arrived at the University of Pittsburgh's library. Dr. Walter Find, another of Mom's old friends, met us there. We were there to see the college's labor union collection.

"Right this way," Walter said, leading us down a hall. "Let me tell you about labor in the United States. The decades right after the Civil War are called the Gilded Age. On the outside, the United States looked wealthy and glitzy. But that hid the ugliness of the poverty that existed here.

Struggling during Tough Times

The United States was in a **depression** during much of the 1870s. Many people were unemployed. For those who did have a job, employers made many of them work long hours for little pay. Most worked 10 to 14 hours a day. Men made up to $1.50 per day."

"Wow, that's not much money at all," I said. "That's like the price of a candy bar today! How could people possibly survive on such low pay?"

"Most laborers struggled to pay for rent, **utilities**, and food," Walter said. "Many wives and children went to work to help out. Children were paid even less. For example, children in a cotton mill made a quarter or two per day! And many mines and mills owned the homes, stores, and schools their laborers used."

"So, the companies controlled employees," I said. "Why didn't the laborers do something about it?"

Workers Strike

"They tried, but if they left their jobs, they'd lose their homes. With all the immigrants coming to the United States, a laborer could be replaced easily," Walter said. "Workers felt helpless. They talked to their coworkers who felt the same way. Many joined unions such as the Knights of Labor. They organized all laborers together to fight for better pay, a safe place to work, and an eight-hour workday. Frustrations boiled over in July 1877 when the Baltimore and Ohio Railroad workers got their second 10-percent pay cut."

"What'd they do about it?" asked Ben.

"The railroad workers in Martinsburg, West Virginia, walked off their jobs, leaving their trains blocking the tracks. Shipping goods and people by rail came to a halt. That would be like semitruck drivers today blocking major highways so no one could get through," he said. "Look at this drawing. What do you think happened next?"

"Looks like there was a big fight," I said. "The bosses must have wanted the trains moved and their laborers back at work."

LABOR DAY

The Labor Day holiday resulted from the labor clashes during the Gilded Age. Laborers were honored with a day to celebrate their achievements. The Central Labor Union's workers celebrated the first Labor Day with a picnic on Tuesday, September 5, 1882, in New York City. Other cities, then other states, celebrated their laborers on that day the next few years. In 1894, the U.S. Congress adopted Labor Day as a national holiday. Since then, it has been held on the first Monday in September.

An artist painted this scene of workers in Martinsburg, West Virginia, blocking the trains during their strike.

"You're right," confirmed Walter. "The governor sent the **militia** to clear the crowd of thousands of people. It was a chaotic scene. Rocks were thrown, shots were fired, and people died. News of what happened spread across the United States. Workers began striking in St. Louis, Chicago, and San Francisco."

"Were there any riots here in Pittsburgh?" I asked.

"Yes. More than 20,000 unemployed workers and striking railroad workers set fire to buildings and railroad cars," Walter explained, pulling out some old newspapers to show us stories.

"Did the strikes help them get paid more?" I asked.

"Unfortunately, no, but it did call attention to the poor working conditions for laborers," Walter said as an announcement came over the loudspeaker stating the library would close in 15 minutes.

"This was very interesting, Walter," Mom said. "We should head to our last vacation stop. Thank you!" ★

Today, we made the final stop on our tour when we arrived in Boston, Massachusetts, and went to Tellie Franklin's home. She's an expert on inventor Alexander Graham Bell. Mom said Bell's work in communication led to industrial growth just as the transportation improvements did.

"Welcome, Elisabeth, boys!" Tellie said. "It's so nice to see you. Please come in my study. I have many Alexander Graham Bell telephone replicas to show you."

Developing the Telephone

"How did Bell come up with the idea for the telephone?" I asked.

"Good question. Bell was a Scottish immigrant whose mother was deaf," she said. "From an early age, he learned to communicate with her using the vibrations of his voice. He taught at Boston's School for the Deaf. During that time, he invented things that could help people, especially the deaf."

"What did he invent?" Ben asked.

"At that time, the only way to communicate over long distances was by telegraph. Messages were made up of dots and dashes in a system known as Morse code," Tellie explained. "In 1874, Bell started working with a builder, Thomas Watson. They planned to make a 'talking telegraph' machine to transmit speech electronically. Look at this drawing. What do you think is going on here?"

"That looks like one person is yelling into a cheerleader's megaphone and the other person is hearing it in another megaphone," I said. "But what are these wavy lines in the middle?"

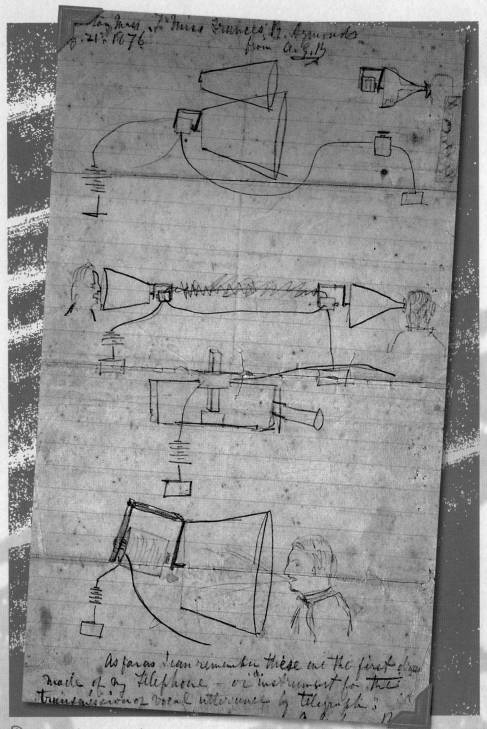

Preservation of this sketch created by Alexander Graham Bell
helps us see how his idea for a telephone started.

"That shows the vibration of the sound from one person to the other through a wire," Tellie said. "The end where he was talking is the transmitter. That machine converted vibrations of his voice to an electric current. The other end is the receiver. That machine turned the electric current back into sound so he could hear what the first person said."

"What was their first conversation?" I asked.

"The first message, on March 10, 1876, was 'Mr. Watson, come here. I want to see you,'" she said. "Watson clearly heard Bell and came running from a nearby room. Their 'instrument for transmission of vocal utterances by telegraph,' known as the telephone today, was a success. Next, Bell needed to sell it."

Making the Telephone Better

"Who would buy such a big machine?" I asked.

"He worked on making it smaller. In June, Bell demonstrated his invention at the **Centennial** Exhibit. People were amazed," Tellie said. "Word spread about his invention. In July 1877, his first

OTHER BELL INVENTIONS

Bell also created a vacuum jacket that was an artificial respirator. It was an early version of the iron lung, which helped people breathe. Bell also invented the audiometer, a device that detects minor hearing problems. Bell was interested in flight, too, and experimented with propellers and kites.

customer wanted a telephone line run from his shop in Boston to his home three miles away. By 1878, there were many other orders for telephones. Telephone poles and lines needed to reach the customers' locations. Now, what do you think is happening in this picture?"

"It looks like some guy is talking into a horn," Ben said.

"No, that's how the telephone looked by October 1892," said Tellie. "That's Bell in New York. He's making the first long-distance telephone call. It was to Chicago."

"Telephones really spread quickly," I said. "The way telephones looked also changed. I can hardly believe my cell phone came from that."

"This has been very interesting, Tellie," Mom said. "Thanks for showing us your collection. It's been quite educational, as has our entire trip."

After we went out to eat with Tellie, we told her good-bye and started our drive home. My travel journal's almost full and I can't wait until next summer's road trip! ★

MISSION ACCOMPLISHED!

You did it! You now understand better the development of industry in the United States. You found out about the transcontinental railroad and its effect on the country and the people in it, including American Indians whose traditional way of life changed dramatically. You learned, too, about the millions of immigrants who came to the United States looking for a fresh start. Many ended up as poor laborers. You studied how workers united and fought for more pay and better working conditions by striking. You discovered how steel was made and how the telephone was invented. Congratulations!

CONSIDER THIS

★ What do you think about allowing immigrants to come freely into the United States?

★ What mode of transportation is equivalent today to the trains of yesterday?

★ If railroad workers were to go on strike today, what do you think would happen? How might you be affected?

★ What do you think it would have been like to be an American Indian in the 1800s?

★ Why do you think people go on strike? Would you ever go on strike?

Trains continue to be used today. Think about
how the railroad affects your life.

GLOSSARY

ancestral (an-SES-truhl) belonging to a person from whom someone is descended

calling (KAWL-ing) a profession, job, or trade

centennial (sen-TEN-ee-uhl) the 100-year anniversary

depression (di-PRESH-uhn) a period of time when business is bad and many people are out of work

immigrant (IM-i-gruhnt) a person who settles in one country after leaving another

impurities (im-PYOOR-i-teez) something that causes the quality of being polluted, harmful, or not pure

militia (muh-LISH-uh) a team of people who have been trained to fight but are not professional soldiers

reservation (rez-ur-VAY-shuhn) a piece of land set aside for a special purpose

spike (spike) a long, thick nail used to fasten heavy lumber on railroads

suspension bridge (suh-SPEN-shuhn brij) a bridge that hangs from cables or chains strung from towers

tenement (TEN-uh-muhnt) an apartment building usually crowded and in a poor section of a city

transcontinental (trans-kahn-tuh-NEN-tuhl) extending across a continent

utility (yoo-TIL-i-tee) a public service such as electricity, water, gas, or telephone

LEARN MORE

BOOKS

DeCapua, Sarah. *Andrew Carnegie*. Ann Arbor, MI: Cherry Lake, 2007.

Landau, Elaine. *Ellis Island*. Danbury, CT: Children's Press, 2008.

Morrow, Ann. *The Gilded Age*. Danbury, CT: Children's Press, 2007.

Patent, Dorothy Hinshaw. *The Buffalo and the Indians*. New York, NY: Clarion Books, 2006.

Perritano, John. *The Transcontinental Railroad*. Danbury, CT: Children's Press, 2010.

WEB SITES

America's Story from America's Library: Gilded Age (1878–1889)
http://www.americaslibrary.gov/jb/gilded/jb_gilded_subj.html
Explore stories about the Gilded Age at this Library of Congress Web site.

Central Pacific Railroad Photographic History Museum
http://cprr.org/
View photographs from the history of the U.S. railroad.

Statue of Liberty-Ellis Island Foundation
http://www.ellisisland.org/
Conduct a passenger search, explore the Immigrant Experience, and learn about the history of this famous place.

FURTHER MISSIONS

MISSION 1

Talk to your parents and grandparents to construct your family tree. Write down when they were born, where they were born, when they were married, and so on. Find out if any of your ancestors came through Ellis Island or the Castle Garden Immigration Station. If so, you could get copies of their ship's passenger list.

MISSION 2

Make a string telephone. Here's what you'll need:

★ two plastic cups

★ two metal paper clips

★ one 10-foot-long piece of string, fishing line, or yarn

★ one thumbtack

★ one friend

Use the thumbtack to poke a small hole in the center of each cup bottom. Tie one end of the string to a paper clip. Push the loose end of the string through the bottom of the cup, keeping the paper clip inside the cup. Slip the string through the bottom of the other cup and tie to the other paper clip. Give one cup to your friend while you hold the other. Pull the string tight. Take turns talking into your cup and listening in the other one!

30

INDEX

ABOUT THE AUTHOR

Mary Meinking grew up spending her family vacations touring the nation in their station wagon. Today, she shares her love of history and travel with her husband, Scott, and two children, Brittany and Benjamin. When Mary's not working as a graphic designer in Iowa, she enjoys writing children's books.

ABOUT THE CONSULTANTS

Brett Barker is an associate professor of history at the University of Wisconsin–Marathon County in Wausau. He received his PhD in history from the University of Wisconsin–Madison and his MA and BA in history from Ohio State University. He has worked with K–12 teachers in two Teaching American History grants.

Gail Saunders-Smith is a former classroom teacher and Reading Recovery teacher leader. Currently, she teaches literacy courses at Youngstown State University in Ohio. Gail is the author of many books for children and three professional books for teachers.